Insert Coin

poems by

Joshua Zelesnick

Finishing Line Press
Georgetown, Kentucky

Insert Coin

Copyright © 2025 by Joshua Zelesnick
ISBN 979-8-88838-834-1 First Edition
All rights reserved under International and Pan-American Copyright Conventions. No part of this book may be reproduced in any manner whatsoever without written permission from the publisher, except in the case of brief quotations embodied in critical articles and reviews.

Publisher: Leah Huete de Maines
Editor: Christen Kincaid
Cover Illustration & Design: Nonpolygon
Author Photo: Jules Carlson

Order online: www.finishinglinepress.com
also available on amazon.com

Author inquiries and mail orders:
Finishing Line Press
PO Box 1626
Georgetown, Kentucky 40324
USA

Contents

LEVEL I.

THE CONTESTANT 1

LEVEL II.

THE OPERATOR 13

TWENTY-THREE HOURS IN SOLITARY 29

LEVEL III.

THE MONSTER 39

LEVEL IV.

THE PRISONER 61

for my mom and dad

for my darlings,
robin
charlotte
violet

AUTHOR'S NOTE

The United States' willingness to torture human beings by locking them in a six-foot by eight-foot cell twenty-three hours a day has everything to do with its capacity to kill indiscriminately by unoccupied aircraft. Not to stop thinking about this, I needed a form.

I found a narrow form of six-syllable lines and eight-line stanzas to reflect the six-foot by eight-foot cell solitary confinement prisoners are forced to live in; I tried to imagine what a consciousness might look like under continual bombardment by the absence of natural light and human contact. This form can be found in the middle section, "Twenty-Three Hours in Solitary."

For the rest of the poetry, which I envision as one long poem with an interruption (the middle section), I tried a strict form of eight-syllable lines and twelve-line poems. Eventually the eight-syllable line gave way.

J.Z. (fall 2020)

"No road to his house, a siege,
And his house is graveyard.
            From a distance, above his house
            a perplexed moon dangles
            from threads of dust."

—Adonis

> david: "is this a game or is it real"?
> joshua/wopr: "what's the difference"?
>
> —from the motion picture, *War Games*

"Click to start. Here is a new world.
The first world opens on a topic."

—McKenzie Wark

LEVEL I.
THE CONTESTANT

a video game in which
the programmers write the code
so detailed that it ends up
covering the territory

exactly, every blade of grass
is accounted for, every house
every shingle on every house
every moon beam

which means every whisper
every last gasp for breath, every
heart that beats again for the
last time is accounted for too

~

bubbling above the waves, GOD'S voice
through a microphone, COME ON DOWN
and in this time lapse our contestant
is born to us, casino bells

and chimes, the clapping crowd, the ears
of our great nation tingling
as we watch the contestant run
down the aisle to produce

our lives, we can't believe her
name was called, and now she's slapping
hands with the other contestants
this who from the crowd will be next

flatten your hand, hold it out front
to end raising suspicion,
take the contestant to the store
and fill her up with thunderous

cheers, press start! the moons of saturn
put us in so much danger, *us*
in the center cannot stop *them*
from holding our fetish is to

colonize, this app opens
the creature's lungs, opens up
the genes, the fabric, the banner
in big bold WHO KILLED PLAYER 1

~

there's a sucker born, is it me
jealous of seeming outsiders
sticking their secret guns in your
gut, of living too much for not much

attention, please there are crumbs
out there, watch them scurry
and wear a helmet, light a torch
blackout in the city, touch it

to reset the system tells us
to take it all, but listen to my heart
translucent with pauses, its bell
stormy with a sliding gate-head

taste my concrescence, these feelings
swim from the rockets' red glare to
simpler launching pads, for what
destruction can offer is great

balance, you never could have guessed
the prisoner living on display
the contestant throwing up, kicked
off the show for taking too much

inside, commercials as threats
BOOM! a force capsized our ship
before we could get to safety
pitted with a sharp edge and tossed

~

if a bank crashes and every
body is around to witness
it, that's meritocracy, our
gallantly streaming video

of asteroids always approaching
our ship rotating in circles
fire, fire, I press the thrust button
forward, but no thrusting back

to the future crowd rallies
at the edifice through the halls
through the shiny acres and scaly
dungeons of it's time to PLAY GAME

hungry as a BANG! BANG!, each
of us with a choice, the sound
of no sound, decisions, decisions
chest high with shadows, soundtrack on

finish your breakfast then begin
the financing, an outpost first
then, BANG! cross your fingers
for a settlement, say

if I could, I'd annex other
planets, say it faster, more confidence
say it with staccato rhythm
say it,   say it,   *let there be light*

~

earth is the right place for liars
longitudes, hyperbole, parks
god's goodness is analogous
to human goodness, what is real

belief if the contestant doesn't
know the rules, circular like breaths
like time to face it—time to take
this face and jam it on there, stick it

on the pike and rally forward
as the crowd cheers with ecstatic
energy can be created
for the sole purpose to destroy

the contestant was abducted
from herself, from her self's self
from her self's self in awe, from her
emptiness, she's got loans, she needs

more time, she needs entertainment
a job that pays, the contestant
is far away from her imagined
self, she's only a contestant in a manner

of speaking, in that any one of us
can be called contestants, in fact she
has from the beginning been a problem
her abducted self the solution, to find

~

just like the caricature
of cecil rhodes with his arms out-
stretched, legs split like a rainbow
left foot planted in cairo, right

foot down to the tip of the cape
in south africa, I too
am a god who straddles between
two extremes and can claim the space

as mine, shotgun on my shoulder
would make it easier, but there is
a difference between him and me
I've only colonized myself

side with the window open looks
remarkable, the view out there
makes me want to remark on its
size, the halves, see all the

realness flaking at the edges
like my dream all night, loud voices
thrusting our surface area
mass creatures stampeding, torrents

toward boundless envy, out there
among the stormy shadows lies
intention, the contestant
without content hope or beauty

~

glory (hole) for the theophany
show us all, broadcast it all, please
for the prisoner, show the images
what do they look like, please what

time does the freedom begin, again
the drone of proof through the night
that his brain is still there, our prisoner
takes refuge in gently touching

his own face to feel some love
follows because it was born here
shaking its head in the river
lake, sea, temple, story, bullet

everything like massive waves
opening eyes, the current is not
too strong or it is, the contestant's feet
in the distance too far to see

what choice did she have but to submit
or not, a ship in the ocean
a ship in space, what difference
does it make where she is in time

floating or thrusting, either are acts
of motion and that's the point
after all, as she saw from the window
the storm and said, *here comes doom doom*

~

saturn possesses a moon that may contain
water, and if this is so saturn's moon may or may
not have exhibited life is what the contestant
thinks to herself, life is round and salty and large and crumbs

and rule of law and warm and curious and debt cycles, life
is stubbed toes and self-help and winter and fudge
and free trade and sour and kissing and which bill to pay
and ponzi schemes, life is extracting fossil fuels

and arbitrage, racist killer cops, and dancing, *does
the moon of saturn present these intricacies*, the contestant
still dressed like a spark white day dream asks, maybe not
she thinks to herself, maybe not this moon

a PAPOOLA, a fox, a pharma
ceutical feeds us ads, but not
without connecting with us first, deep
emotional to our most vulnerable

form of self help, soothing and coaxing
the small insect tells us it loves
us as much as we love it because
let's face it, everybody loves

a pet guiding us in all
the directions we should need to go
if only we had the will
to buy, to spend, to change

~

*because women are interesting
and important,* said
the contestant to the eager
audience awaiting the moment

to applaud, *they are not an after
thought, not secondary players
in human destiny and we
have always known that,* which is why

the contestant was speaking
without the future tense, without
some sickness to possess, chewing
up language to fuse to the chatter

she falls through a hole
into a special bonus level
on one of the moons of saturn
quiet like the inside of a wave

craters that seem to change
color in the pearl-soft mists
her voice sings little blue bird
secrets like a hook that can drag eyes

backward, she never forgets
to reset her patterns, mythical
trends that reveal some disturbing
clichés related to her desire to become

~

when she crawls inside herself
an orange falls down from her hand, and as it
drifts toward the hole that has opened below her
she falls through, and the orange is still falling

somewhere, and she is falling too, except she can't
see the orange, and as far as she can tell
the orange is still there, but she can't see it
she crawls inside herself and thinks another orange

has fallen, but she can't see it, another hole opens
below her, but she can't see it, she keeps falling below
herself, but she is in the oranges and somewhere is in
the holes falling through the oranges somewhere

—*to Frank O'Hara*

LEVEL II.
THE OPERATOR

in the river, what rises in the river
is nothing, in the river rises nothing
there it rises and rises
in the river who rises there, the operator

there rises the drone, the operator
there it rises he rises, TARGET
now burn for you, and your eye, whereto
rises your eye, your eye rises

opposite the river, your eye
a window, rises opposite the river
expands to cover bodies burned to cinder
a window, your eye collecting   footage

—*to Paul Celan*

~

the operator thought it was the coolest
damn thing, to play video games
all day, just point and click
and his player never dies, but it wasn't

like flipping a switch, the war never
goes away, could never ask a therapist
for help because they'd take his security
clearance, but a chaplain

more often than not would say, *it's all part
of god's plan* to kill the first time was horrible,
the second time was horrible, the third time
was numbing, the fourth time, numbing

weary of make believe, bodies
bursting in air remote
controlled night and day by heroes
with pixilated weapons of mass

listen to the fabric in that
something exists, catch a human
by the hair over the rampart
scene, constructing walls can't defend us

from our tectonic heart
beats our fingers on controls, PLAY
take this delirium of star
spangled static and thrust it hard

~

in the control room, a photo
from september 11th, the second
plane hitting the second tower
as motivation, pissed off all

over again right before we're
charged to kill, a voice: *these guys deserve
to die,* but I don't think I can fire,
well, you swore an oath, so legally

a portal opens to absorb
my light, like the tower absorbed
the plane, just sucked it in the chest
full speed and never let it out

secret patterns of behavior
you're in war, you're out of war, you're
in war, you're the operator
the ultimate peeping tom

seen and unseen in the friendly
skies, a riddle across dimensions,
oceans, deserts, the drone is there
see it clearly in the sky, but

what of the pilot eight thousand
miles away, in an office portal
to reach through, a silhouette
to see through a face obscured

~

the drone operator is sick
his disease, can't see faces
too much shooting at targets, windows
in the ground, what distant planet

would zero in and FIRE, sickness
of a building rocking inside his cockpit
zeroing in with precision, great american
heroes put the air in air power

look at him, he has gone too long
without seeing for real, doesn't recognize me
walks right past *that body's moving and it's
a real live crawling boy*, ROGER THAT

who's there, the BANKS level
so where you gonna run to
there's nowhere left
the gutter, the gutter, I'll hide

in the gutter, no, banks own the
gutters, so where you gonna
run to, *the woods, the woods, I'll hide
in the woods,* nope, no use banks own

the trees now, so where you gonna
run to, *the stars, the stars, I'll hide
with the stars,* okay, but you'll have to pay
thirty percent interest,   a day

~

space dwells in all of us, the kick
of freedom with its border
cracks connect a constellation
that swells to a fire

the contestant couldn't put out
sits opposite the operator for a chat, a rush
of ideas that amount to an omen
that trickles down their cords

says the contestant, *where there once
was hope, there is absence*
the operator offers back
where there is absence there is a carcass

pocket-sized black holes, 90's era
in good condition awaiting
just the right customer
before they're discarded along

with the hubble telescope that
discovered them, and what a deal
of the century, your purchase
includes the story of their origin

a dark place to be sure, and even though
they are quite small, they are still effective,
these black holes, which are
all different in shape but not outcome

—to Emilio Adolfo Westphalen

~

the enemy is a monster
is the basic idea
of practically every war
mythology, we invade

from the air so we don't see
the monster's face mounted, the wall
between heaven and hell, little
pouches to collect their breaths

a little shrine to collect
our thoughts for the last time again
I want to become a robot, I
don't want to become a robot, I

go on   an odyssey, in arcade years,
lasts all night, a video game
is just a death, avatars trapped
in the afterlife bear witness

to the bells and chimes of an
outmoded form this dream
of infinite lives, friends, feelings
that burst out like a pinball

around a loop, sirens, screeching
brakes, motors, the shrill of fighter
jets locking in, I'm bewitched
by memory on a spinning track

~

this fabrication of cosmos
can once and for all pluck me to
bear witness, my march song, madness
to the lists that disguise themselves

as freedom to articulate
my only voice, *glass,* I am not
equipped to make the decisions
required, so I hop from rock

to rock to avoid the snakes, *hiss*
only two lives left, more *hiss,* so jump
over the edge, I make my choice
in this space of daydreams   APPLAUSE

maybe we're all just time soldiers
aiming our guns with eight-way
rotary joysticks, walking
in one direction, while shooting

in another, we re-enter
the portal until we arrive
at the correct time period,
THE AGE OF WAR, and out we pop

to shoot our enemies along
a scrolling backdrop, but this
can't be LIFE, unlimited
on all levels, except the last

~

six thousand twenty year olds
deployed in place on the ops floor
spying, could be called reapers, dimly
lit room, arcade-style, streaming

footage from drones circling battlefields,
I saw blood so precise the missile took
the father, but not the
child walked back to the pieces

of his father and began to place the pieces
back into human shape, crouching low
in the hollow of a gully with no door or window
to pull, just the horizon, lumps, angst-colored

gravitas at the end at the
hand of our CEASAR, harkens birds
and dreamscapes, the fabric opens
hail, hail the lucky ones, design

spaces to live to relocate
in case of encountering the
monsters in you in me in what
is this blockade and search, promise

to touch gently our privates and
not lose sense of feeling ever
that lightness as it raptures up
up, up, up, up—can you feel it

~

enough with positive thinking
parts of the whole cannot replace
whole parts that cannot, be in me
drown my barbie smile, sergeant says

*suck the bone from the suck the fuck
up son,* face the fountain with my
coin, knife, shiny instrument of
blind spots, not knowing what I don't

know, that there must be a better—
*what you don't know is a function
of what you know*—way to express
my end is coming and I'm pissed

DAJIANG INNOVATIONS OWNS 70 percent
AEROVIRONMENT is a world leader
AMBARELLA produces video
processing chips, BOEING a drone

that's launched via catapult, GO PRO's karma
is most popular, LOCKHEED MARTIN
engineering a better tomorrow
GENERAL ATOMICS'S MQ-9 has reapered

more civilians than any other
3-D ROBOTICS equals smart
NORTHROP GRUMMAN's earnings are expected
to grow 12 percent this year, what about next

~

do you hear that buzz around
town is to invest before it's too
late, the mega-trend phenomenon
is here to stay today and on

into the future, so come to claim
your slice without the pie
predicted thick and juicy will
capture the fancy of many

drone manufacturers have
replicated the theories
of sci-fi movies and books
to give birth to real, screams

tips would be appreciated
between my tits are on live stream
with our flag still planted in space
can be expanded, let's make room

for my heart, pet, prisoner
all squeeze into frame, the
prisoner digs a hole as a home
to keep the sun off, digs through

dead volcanoes, craters
and lava flows, it was always dark
eventually a cough, catches
fever first fast and passes it on

~

I am not anti
religion, but I am
against selling thunder
at the crossroads, buying gunnery

to seize control of an anthem
and then we're all forced into
costumes that show our ranks
in order of appearance

player 1, bank robber, heretic
correlates to the creation
of weaponry through the long
twenty-first century,   *can I get an* A...

the difference between death and
video games is lives left, or
how many fantasies do the drone
victims have left, this level

begins and ends with a target
is my name, see my I.D. says
TARGET a silhouette before
trial, the joystick vibrates

through the clouds, the order
YOU'RE CLEARED TO FIRE, but what if
voices leaving an arcade, mega
pixels picking okra in a field

~

crosses loomed over the roman
empire to warn people that they
could be killed whenever—
nose cone, two wings and a tail

can't hide from the crucifixion
no god, just PILATES
recycled over and over
in their cockpits of chain command

prefects from JUDEA
to DC, they encircle, share
secrets serene through the crosshairs
the empire is a gravedigger

the capacity to die as he stares
at his foe, some eyeless creature
that has evolved in dark corners, nose
cone blunt and featureless

on the horizon, the real
difference is life, potential calm
DAVID without armor, on the run
with sling, fires! the smooth stone

sinks deep into the skull of
fiber-reinforced composite
that isn't *real*
doesn't breathe, doesn't die

~

take advantage of one or both
great offers, everyone agrees
either will end up screwing
you in your private   ization

frenzy, your so-called creative
community is exclusive
to variety, pick your choice
from ten models, bonus one

wish, the sole motivator for
war happens when sharp-edged plastics
feel threatened, the complex weakens
and followers hatch out, like toys

why do you think a drone is called
a drone, *the sound* is what
everybody thinks, but no
it's named after the drone bee

hatched from drone eggs to serve
a single purpose impregnate
the queen, after which it dies
noble and mindless, its eyes

twice the size of the worker bee
in order to zoom-in and mate
mid-air with its target, grasps on with all
six legs, the penis gets ripped from the body

~

to build an arcade is simple
lungs, fabricated engines, time
capsule inside children, line up
over your target and drop

a bouquet of bombs when they hit
yell, SPLASH and the bodies
blow, parts of the whole next level
of forgiveness, like where's the secret

whistle that skips me ahead, how
many lives do I have left, if
we stay here all night how much
would it cost to beat the whole game

TWENTY-THREE HOURS IN SOLITARY

all our separations
have been learned, like when I
heard a sharp clear echo
in the birth canal that
sounded like the zooming
of a lens, pulled into
existence, I was—in
this world, but not of it

entombed *I* for who knows
secrets of the state, this
poem is more than just
collisions, a series
on repeat more than a
shiver at sea, than my
hands vibrating on cold
bars never open up

the illusion bell rings
from the illusion cell
thoughts like weapons passing
in the night, terrors spring
out, this cave on repeat
how many times can you
force me to say, I'm a
prisoner, I don't deserve

light, to censor feelings,
stand (up)! slowly step away
from the empire, *state your
name* for the record book
number of screams this year!
I'm not an animal
you are an animal
I'm blended particles

lion-hearted purpose
is why I'm here! promise
I won't create my own
universe of diverse
pixels in the garden
I squeeze tomatoes plump
on the vine and watch with
wonder each explosion

like a bomb! flashes like
how else to explain but
I'm in a video
game and there's no way out
I see the swaying tail
the monster's fuzzy skin
multiple monsters, so
I run from doom, I run

(and) all I can do is hide
am I in the walls, no
I'm in the air, shot through
the gut, that's why I fall
so quickly, why all this
energy goes through me
why I stare at a shard
of glass, lift, then swallow

on my axis, I bow
should I find the law for
this slovenly score with-
in me, should history
have a sugary smell
my home demolished, so
I flee, a refugee
crisis in THE JUNGLE

and then there was darkness
is a virtue—*say light*
a thousand times every
morning and you never
know, a wish can grow like
flowers from the brain, a
little water every
day between breaths—then buds

their lawyers said it was
legal, so *they* did it
light deprivation, cells
inside my body shocked
back to myth, TANTULUS
blindfolded upside down
saw creation was all
around us, saw me—my

head under water for
a limited time, I
imagine MICKEY MOUSE
without a trial, hanging
fruit to savor along
side the collateral
damage, I was always
here to collect   footage

can smell it nasty stuff
piles up so high looks like
a de Chirico, glass
statues, burnt wood, trains, I
replace the hopeless crunch
of guards' heals outside my
SHU with the sound of star
glow, busting through the vines

this fountain of truth makes
me thirsty for even
more fountains, more hormones!
I too am a tree just
like we all are, outside
we climb black branches up
trunks to peak out at the
war on women franchise

selling like trickle down
chocolate cake, I suck on
the spoon all afternoon
if only I could make
commission off that, if
only I could fall a-
sleep communing with stars
become part of the WHOLE

this machine kills hope of
the infinite, just one
more chase scene inside the
situation room, then
I smile slightly to show
I recognize evil
is happening to me
underground with the bugs

can hear them crawling one
on top of the other
darkness of night as soft
as a song if one knows
how to listen proper,
I think indefinite
detention is like thoughts
reflected on water

the water does not get
broken, nor my thoughts wet
my thoughts are wide,
yet the entirety
of all of my thoughts can
be reflected even
on a single drop, part
of the whole, whole part of

not a thou, but a thing,
an IT, like digging a
hole straight down the middle
of the ocean with a
shovel made of water
this is how I feel most
days, like what if MOSES
never even split the sea

rock-hard mattress I rip
a hole in, crawl inside
as if I am a slug,
as if death is something
I can create with my
own hands, but there is no
exit strategy from
here, just god on one side

and self-mutilation
on the other, so I
ask god, which way out, then
a door swings open to
the beyond, an azure
void, *should I walk through*, I
ask, but nobody is
ever there to answer

tragedy happens through
me not to me, six by
eight walls that close to a
crush, a glut of specters
my mind removed to a
point outside the body
like a beautiful star
a shield to consider

to be planted like grass
in a box as the earth
revolves, a walk along
a cliff's edge reveals my
self falling back up from
my death to start again
this nothingness never
was, it's me! so I breathe

beloved, ghost ship on
the horizon, DEATH and
DEATH-IN-LIFE play dice for
my soul, but I never
shot an albatross, could
never shoot anything,
not even myself, *here*
I am, come and get me

LEVEL III.
THE MONSTER

what theory launched us toward the parade
what wicked light shot its angle toward our
gaze, it's just a tango all these children leaving
the arcade with stuttered steps and marching

toward the parade, ascending above the market
place, descending all these children weary
and afraid, what about the sounds, images
on screens, too much flashing light can lead a child

insane to feed off things that move
off guts and bloody scenes, it's a tango
marching wounded toward the parade
all these children leaving the arcade

~

the prisoner is a hologram
can you tell, the glow, and we should
all take comfort in that reality
that even though there is no body now

the hologram still speaks eloquently
almost as eloquently as the prisoner
in the flesh once spoke, which is cause enough
for optimism don't you think

getting irritated at the reporter
for probing about false connections the hologram
says, *look, I'm getting annoyed*, see how
on point, as on point as any hologram could be

let's invite the monster, a heartache may follow
but it only hurts when it crawls out of the ache
and pounds, the idea of the monster is only
my idea of the monster and none of my ideas

are entirely my own, forever wishing and hoping
cannot change the realness of the image, for instance
when the soldiers came in, the monster let them
and they stayed, how long can a group stay in a place

that isn't theirs, they asked the monster for input
on a matter, so the monster gave some shoddy input and they
whisked the monster away to a dark place with long corridors
that led to a vanishing point, torch lights,   a vast plain

~

my social media feed reads *insert coin
to continue,* but there is no
where to do this, so solely out
of habit I post, *the sun rises*

as a manner of what else but
panic, as a way to adapt, to
practice holding a hand firm
or loose is learned at an early

age, like why do bodies come with
organs or a sky full of drones
these divisions spiral to a blur
with no narration, only noise

in solitary, research proves
difficult to pull through the bars
all day, a desk, the archive, fever
from no natural light source

our prisoner is hyper active, scanned
into this secret glow
the slightest motion could upset
the landscape, and then erase

his dewy eyes, covered from view
with 3-d glasses—lighting up
I reach toward the cold shadow
of a cloud to pull down the blinds

~

the split body, parts
can see me in the mirror
full length, but with two faces
one paler than the other

like lincoln, it bothered him
ill in bed, he got up it vanished
but when he lay back down
there in the glass again were two

faces, the tip of the nose of one
three inches from the tip of the nose
of the other, his wife said an omen
of death, behind the curtain, buzzing

the drone operator dreamed his
head was caught in a freezer
ice even dropped on it, sometimes
just one at a time, sometimes 5-7

like bullets in a row, the operator
thought it was strange what they felt like
dropping on the back slab of his
head, but actually they felt just

like bodies falling on the back
flap of the head, what weight he had
to carry, he rocked from left to right
reloaded, left to right, reloaded, left to

~

the victims prefer gray skies
prefer rain all day all
gray out like a stone they can pull
back and slingshot at the drones

gray, the color of life, drones
don't fly when gray skies, when think
about visibility, when
for a short time mental tension

and fear eases, when the world
in reverse sneaks up to correct
itself once again the sky brightens
and with it the trembling, the terror

the operator's feed is too grainy
choppy, a child or a chicken
terrorist, insurgent, no
an opera singer, hear that voice

spreads disease requiring quarantine
as in banned from the state
destroyed doesn't quite capture
the ruination like destructed does

clocks that wind backwards to show us
again who we really are and will
surely recognize a meme
in the mirror, wrecking ball

~

in the world that does exist
this book can't end, except
through science fiction, an exploding
star I draw as my self-portrait—

all of us drawing self portraits
in the world that does exist, two
common eyes, mouth, two ears so full
of sound twisting my recurring

dream becomes the world, I'm forced
to sit in a chair and watch
the violence, when I try to move
my head gets jerked back to place

I'm still utterly
terrifyingly human
after all, I still have bones and
heat and a little wheel that turns

toward the glow of monitors
midwinter landscape
a palette of grays and browns, fields
cut to stubble, dark forests climbing

the rocky foothills, three men, then
the directive: *confirmed weapons*
three…two…one…I say, *missile off
the rail,* screen lit up with white flash

~

around the corner we will all
just go away, trip the lever
that was advertised to protect us
and fall to the mighty, sorry

they will say—just that accidents
happen, only trying to save
our company's life is precious
too, I ran the numbers and found

THAT'S A WEAPON! so i move
to the side and the anvil
falls through the floor, keeps falling
floor after floor after floor

but she is in the oranges and
somewhere is in the holes, falling with
the oranges somewhere, the contestant
tries to fall through the oranges

but the holes crawl into themselves
she knows she's falling somewhere
and the holes are in the oranges but she
can't see herself, the holes   are falling

through her, the oranges are falling
through the oranges, and she
crawls into the holes, falls with
the oranges but they can't see her

~

strange electronic limbo, white
hot clarity of nightmare
in infrared, heat signatures
ghostly white against the cool black

earth, a little cam show reflection
reveals fascists removed
expression from museums
to control how much we feel

down, way down to where the ocean
meets the soul floods us all with light
rises to where the eyes, there's no mistake
look! the eyes are windows, screams!

the contestant has been placed
in orbit, plugged in, satellized,
what if anything
is real about her or this land

worth sailing to, superficial
saturation and fascination
her gestures will soon be
obsolete, the earth collapsing

in on us, everything automated
the game show host ossifies
on air   absorbs all color
almost a stiff, spooks us

~

eight-second window to divert
the missile once off the rail
the operator counts individual
pixels on the monitor, suddenly

two seconds, a child walks around
the corner, *one,* the digital screen
flickers to the real, parts
of the dwelling collapse, no

child there, *was that a kid,* he asks
then a voice anywhere in the world, *no
that was a dog* REPLAY he sees
again, the horror   two legs

little things that we can even
tually do for immediate
help will eventually fan
out into larger bigger helps

I believe that and hold to its
parody of humanism—
for instance, a perilous fight
births parades, some bodies

don't count the same as others
accidents in the foma
real truth can be expressed, narrowed
by switching sides, ways to listen

~

if the operator enters the drone
hangar, the official inside will beat him
he wants to enter because he suspects
the hangar is holding his heart

and he wants to try to fly it for real
but he saw another drone
operator enter and when that operator
entered, he heard him get beaten

bad, thumps and breathing
like a dry rattling of a shutter
some splashing water and then
as if by a switch, no noise

in this cartoon the body weighs
exactly, it's real, my secret
self, the monster's twilight
as he climbs clouds to challenge

creation, up there, high up there
the drone in the stars, looks down
at the contestant, fidgety
as she prepares to go on stage

god is changing with the times
forever expanding naked
for the viewer, wearing only
a spark with the scent of ISAAC

~

the monster is a viceroy
for change, the code for it
archived like a map
that becomes the territory

the monster becomes the territory
reconstructed in vitro
so therefore kept secret from even
the mother, earth come to ask once more

if I was returning to enjoy
the seasons and not to hurry
if I wasn't, maybe only
along for the ride back to the glow

DESTROYED doesn't quite capture the
ruination like DESTRUCTED
does, it can take as long as
how many seconds between

the *cleared hot* and the hell fire
SPLASH, veneers of houses torn off
into toys, I ask again, *a child
or a chicken*, no, a dark field

with swirling dots, an amulet
to refocus the lens ask
what does it mean to be alive, ask
what does it mean my *last exit*

—to Solmaz Sharif

~

when astronomers say we're not far
off from colonies on the moon
all I can think about is how
many acres will be covered

with concrete, that once again
we will have succeeded at
spreading the ache, the shape
of a wall smoothed by a trowel

*the universe is mostly
empty space after all*
the ad will play, *we should
need to fill it with something*

a patriot high
on his perch in the
nevada desert responds
to a text, *can you stop for milk*

on his way home
comes to a light, a four way
the light doesn't change, *it won't*
stays red, a reflection

on the ground of every
other light turns green
except his
stays red

~

so I stuff a quarter down the slot
but that's not enough anymore,
so I stuff another quarter
down and off to never never

land, where memory little by
little resembles the thickness
of clouds that say *exit light*! or
take my hand, or go gather evidence

*for the wedding party defense
program*, I mistook a camera
for a gun and nobody cared, no body
but me, brain flash to the bulb

pioneer, hunter, dragon
eye, hawk pointer, dessert hawk
predator, gray eagle, global
hawk, shadow, fire scout, coyote

reaper, snowgoose, raven, wasp
crossbow, puma, pegasus, blackjack
sentinel, black hornet, snipe
switchblade, maveric, stalker

scaneagle, triton, stingray, gnat,
hellfire, phantom, condor, polecat
hummingbird, darkstar, sea ghost, king
fisher, scorpian, dominator

~

the future is here, and it's
lunar, concrete could be useful
for sculpting structures on the moon,
especially when colonization

occurs, sulfur-based LUNAR CONCRETE
is the way to go due to the abundance
of sulfur and the ill-abundance of water
although this isn't a problem

for all moons, like the moons
of saturn, it is a problem for our
moon, so sulfur as a binding agent
is essential to our future, manifest destiny

unexpected challenges often
occur at the most inopportune
times, so reach for your milestone
master card and smile like a daisy

surrounded by other daisies
in a field so full of daisies
nicknamed for today only THE FIELD
OF DAISY DELIGHT, *this could be you*

says the papoola, unsecure
less than perfect credit, funniest
little things happening all around you
pet me to get pre-qualified

~

*I'm finished with talking to you
as a human recreation
pack*, explains the contestant
dressed tightly in her human face

dressed again securely in her
game show slacks, dressed again within
the bells and chimes, and again with
scraps of total paranoia

reaches for a metaphor—
a machete and decapitates
the host right there, live
the audience just hums

a virus hereafter referred to as
ROTABANK, a gastroenteritis
caused by our bodies full of
JPEGS and transmitted orally

through incalculable clichés, but
that's not what the ad will play as
I sit losing my shiny
temper a bank is never built

it remains a flicker stored
in our minds, recall
is everything, the city excretes
tiny estates, gates, swerving into

~

you show up to a public hearing
where many people have already
assembled, a gentle raucous vibrates
the great hall circular, one by

one denizens approach
the mic to give testimony
each unique, grievances imperfect
even a few fingers point

ecstatically to express, but
instead of officials tucked neatly
up front, there is a screen, a video
playing on a continuous loop

white bags of AMMONIUM NITRATE
at a homemade explosives factory turns
out to be bags of cotton at a gin, terrorist
HEADQUARTERS is actually the longtime

home of two brothers, their wives and children
ADULT MALE associated with terrorists is
an elderly female, a HEAVY OBJECT being dragged
into a building is in fact a child, males on

motorcycles driving quickly in FORMATION are just
teens on motorbikes, ten children playing near the target
structure classified as TRANSIENT are eating
dinner when rock and concrete crush down

~

hellfire AGM-114A, INTERIM hellfire
semi-active laser homing, hellfire II
w/elctro-optical countermeasures
hellfire LONGBOW *fire and forget* millimeter

wave radar seeker coupled with inertial
guidance homing capability in adverse
weather, hellfire II BLAST FRAG for bunkers, light
vehicles, and caves, hellfire MAC w/metal

augmented charge, hellfire UAS for all
surface targets, hellfire ROMEO w/reduced net
explosive weight, hellfire R9X FLYING GINSU w/pop
out blades for crushing and slicing humans

the operator flies along
the pathway of a dark wound
never treated, today is about
remembering

the lightness of their hands, soft
sounds, utterances from there
to here, promises kept along
the way, and passages squeezed

through, the dusty edge
where the world explodes
again and again without even
a discussion, in the morning

~

I confess to you my sins
petal-shaped around the edges
as a way to escape
my big and ugly center

what happens when the risks
are entirely one-sided
keeps repeating in my head
can hear the stone and dirt collapse

glass from windows all of it
scratch into each other
until finally a pile, as if
an asteroid drifts by, wipeout

shimmy-shimmy denial days
last a long time to watch the
minstrel show, I'll be packing my things
brain, soul-shine, questions, three-day-pass

if only answers were enough
I'm trapped in my speech
patterns become the easiest
way to communicate without

worry of misunderstandings
happen when two or more parties
confront each other with their own
predictability, will say

~

living room cockpits of complicity
we hear the headline, *stocks surge
after missile attack,* a drop
to the bottom like a prescription

bottle, burnt orange, is thrown away
with not even an afterthought, no
discussion of heritage first
just popped balloons before

they're even filled with air, what axis
of thought could accept such timing
breathing in breathing out, breathing
the order, *light 'em all up*

ACTION 26.9 percent, SHOOTER
20.9 percent, ROLE PLAYING 11.3
percent, SPORT 11.1 percent
ADVENTURE 7.9 percent

FIGHTING 7.8 percent, RACING
5.8 percent, STRATEGY 3.7
percent, OTHER 4.6 percent,
take your time, these are the sales

by genre, ACTION 26.9 percent
SHOOTER 20.9 percent, SHOOTER
20.9 percent, SHOOTER 20.9
percent, SHOOTER 20.9

~

good banking is good citizen
shipwrecked without a safety boat
again, and the waves are almost
too much to take a look at me

my bobbing ears, I'm not
in the drone, my heart drenched, filling
with soggy future, its bell gone
deaf in its place, just a humming

cover my head and force me where
heroes get too big to fall, I could
only win when I climbed back
down the stalk to earth, no more

LEVEL IV.
THE PRISONER

the contestant enters but what she thinks
will be different chairs are after
all the same chair
one after another, so what does she do

you could have guessed is continue
to sit in them, only none seem
better than the other, so what
does she do is tastes a little

porridge from all the bowls
only each is still too hot, so
when she gets to the beds she's so full
of angst, she just leaves, no trace

~

how to establish PATTERN OF LIFE
with the use of extraordinary
technology, on the day of the planned
strike, three children climbed up

onto the roof, I can still see their
shadows in front of me, zoom out
flat circular disk is our galaxy
and we're in it, my voice

is cracking now, the children would go
up to the roof when they got cold
on the roof there was an oven, on the roof
they could warm up under the sun

buried under a debris of words
militant, lawless, terrorist, compound
how can a weapon be called accurate
pinpoint when it has a kill

radius of fifty feet
wounding radius sixty-five
did you hear it coming, no
says the prisoner, I was

knocked out, the conversation
begins with a prosthetic
leg, a glass eye, *I* was
cleaning dishes after dinner

~

the prisoner in a t-shirt
the prisoner in a blazer
the prisoner with make-up
hair slicked just so, the camera's twitch

the prisoner in the embassy
the prisoner in solitary
the prisoner with sleep-deprived
eyes still pale as a suffocating

fish, the prisoner in the breeze
the prisoner climbing trees
the prisoner as a meme, planted
in the parched earth with dramatic lighting

bar graph sliding down to nothing
characters are not people
in a world that appears as a vast
accumulation of images

the pleasure in destroying characters
to demonstrate again and again
their worthlessness, our suffering
prisoner turns to face the gamer

looking out toward an absent sky
appealing directly beyond
the frame of the game itself
as if cursing god, and I am god

~

titanfall 2, battlefield 1
counter-strike global offensive
call of duty modern warfare
battlefield 4, call of duty

black ops III, sniper elite, call
of duty advanced warfare, tom
clancy's the division, tom clancy's
rainbow six siege, tom clancy's ghost

recon wildlands, sniper elite III,
ultimate edition, battlefield
hardline, call of duty infinite warfare
killing floor, call of duty ghosts

when the prisoner looks up at the flag
all he sees is a dead body, we've
come a long way since SPACEWAR
since DUCK HUNT, since BATTLEZONE and DOOM

first-person shooters have been funded
by the pentagon since WW II
the crowd stands to honor fallen heroes
brought to you by RAYTHEON, guiding

missiles to the heart since 1948
you hear that thump, you know you're alive
soldier player 1, soldier player 2
this trailer shoots down aircraft with microwaves

~

I still have things to say in this
holding pattern, eons
are short, the young actor
almost starts WW III by playing

a video game, START
the armada appears, our ship
still rotating in circles, moments
seem endless, *Joshua what are you doing*

the professor whispers as flashes
of scenarios play out too fast to process
for a human, the computer's deduction
the only winning move is not to play

an app to colonize the stars
the next generation could all
be holograms, light against
shadow creates what, roadkill

for one, maybe global economic
growth, laws, more mining nightmares
on the moons of saturn, choking
beyond the slow sweep of a hand

there is a flag easy to move
from our moon to another
to another, to all places
none of us should ever see

~

game not over until you win
your reward for jamming
more quarters down the shoot
out with the polarity machine

has been on play for two (plus) centuries
the prisoner moves forward from the PARIS
COMMUNE, the right to the city
belongs to the contestant

with no annual fee, proudly
she hoists her bonus points above
her tilted body like a tombstone
that briefly proves she lived   or died

jumping out windows requires
high velocity and constant ~~animation~~
ammunition, steer clear of the kinetic
warhead with pop-out blades, its weight

exactly 45 kg of
six knives flying at high speeds
to cut and crush causing minimal
collateral damage, such parables are taught

like maps to our youth, the contestant
knew how to swing her face in view for the close-up
as a way to ask, *does the soul then*
have to stay, yes it does, with the body, for now

~

how can I give a sense of who
the contestant is as a human
because originally she was
caricature, a voice to become

our collective cry in the lost
exhale, because that is what
I was most interested
in showing, to gobble

up and spit out as a
kind of joke because
ha, ha, the joke is on all of us
because *ha, ha*

in the river, make believe bodies
a portal opens toward the parade
all these children leaving
the arcade, up on rooftops

to get warm, all these children
weary and afraid, what about
their shivering hands pushed to the sun
the camera magnifies [redacted]

playing near the target structure
a child or a chicken, a vast plain
this was not an error, all these
children were included in the raid

~

terror as an assembly line
refrain, who looks in and who
looks out ~~windows~~ screens is actually
only one way of looking,　OUT

how to look back into the camera
becomes the subject of the new
documentary series, a scream
like script I am hinting at, banks,

exxon, teledyne, et al don't give
a damn about you, just *push murder
paper around all day,* we see *here*
a coup, *there* a coup,　clicks into place

the operator refuses
the bonus, points upward and says
what level is this, below the clouds
there's a bubbling of

WHIRR sounds! could be an attack
so which way to go when nowhere
when *god damn you*! this is
the mirror level!

images appear then
disappear, cling on, laser
accurate penetration
to the soul, shaped like an eye

~

manipulating the LIBOR rate
is as natural as the operator
honing in on a home
where in the courtyard tulips

are about to bloom, the pleasure
in launching the missile, then
watching the target burn must be similar
to the pleasure of knowing

you secretly raised the cost of
a home by raising the cost of everything
honing and homing the green futures
market of war footage

a cloud that follows us
wherever we go, what is lost
our auras, our mothers
fathers stripped and humiliated

in the middle of the street
remote pilot opens a window
to feel the breeze, notices
the contestant in high def

a look of worry at the wheel
as time runs out
the audience explodes
into the future collateral damage

~

stark, dark, unforgettable
tv ad, robots, spiders, scripts
scrapers, crawlers, ants, scutters,
arachnid, spindle, grunk, aperture,

hounder, harvesting, greese monkey,
node, phantom, wrangling, wrapping,
importer, firebug, or any
automated or manual

equivalent to mine the archive
one of these should work, like what do
you want to find, the *collateral murder* video
black sites, humvees, the real location of julian assange

I think money's been a really
disappointing thing, I can't eat
this tulip bulb craze the cynic
knows the price, your castle, how

much logic tends to peak the value
in the air will outlast the shine
these fancy stripes or flames, you crave
a bubble but can't afford

the bus fare, to history, yourself
in the leap, the prisoner has a dream
to invade from under the city, a huge
umbrella cracking the pavement

~

everything looks familiar
none of the traps or tricks surprise
me, which way to go since the dawn
panoramic shots of cityscapes

the prisoner travels
through the birth canal only
to reawaken to the entire
world as a BATTLESPACE

around-the-clock tracking
persistent stares from the tyranny
of the unblinking eye in orbit
to FIND, FIX, and FINISH him

do you enjoy the night sky
as it is, beautiful glittery gems
from galaxies far away, the
occasional UFO that turns out

to be STARLINK brining internet
even to the middle of the ocean … well now,
imagine a certain drone operator
with a certain imagination

to gather all the drones of warfare
and fly them remotely off the planet
to form a single constellation
with a singular message

~

a picture of a child's face enlarged
and secured to the roof for the drones
to see on what level, in which
world, by whom, how many

civilians taken by the crater
in the center, whose mind
was made up, the wind was coming
from what direction, if I told you

once, I told you the time
is now, it's about time, it goes
by so fast, but it's slow, we don't
have enough THIS is our time

who gave the orders
who obeyed the orders
who formed the bank
who robbed the bank

should be put on trial crimes
committed every day, and what
justice for killing one mother
compared to killing a thousand

looking for blood vengeance
that is always looming
a tidal wave, flash
of pixels, perplexed moon

~

in the dark, the prisoner lines
up cockroaches out of sheer
boredom, thinks, *maybe a circle,*
this time *a game of dominos*

challenges himself to spell words
at first, then phrases, sentences
writhes the crusty constellations
off his torso, neck

a flick of the hand, a manifesto
as a crowd gathers at the edifice
through the halls, at the video game's
distressed edge blinking GAME OVER!

another apocalypse ride
down the mountain
with a hawk's eye view, I notice
specks of glass, rocks, a ring

of swifts swerve, a murderer
in blurry air, my
future a buzzing flower out
of reach, harsh weather, harsh dream

this time my face looks out
toward a pattern home
to rescue my feelings
from the chest of this peak, inside

~

the sky and ocean are reverses
of each other, gaze at one
take a dagger to the other
this scenic view goes viral

just like that, snap
clouds blacken, sand
rallies with the wind loosens
all the shells, then what, a gale

then what, a conspiracy
to give the illusion of a flood
walk backwards away from the water
and watch the buildings disappear

I emerge from darkness as a pet
leader to take the temperatures
of crowds exhausted, cracked and spooned
little fish never eat big fish

yet, do you see on set
the contestant would like
to make it a true daily double
before she's reassured to sink

underground with her coffin
whispers sweet stillness, hides
away, to start anew downward
purpose, anew kind light

~

stripped and planted, his body
absorbs every last lumen of sun
so lush the prisoner senses
the screech of each pore

sprouts among his arms and shoulders
his neck stretches to the point
of moving beyond, squeezing out
of the only place he had the right

to belong, a remaking
of the self as an abstract
topiary with prisoner limbs
germinating from cinder blocks

are we separate from the target
have we merged with the target
if the prisoner is the target
is it possible to merge

with him in such a diminutive
space, to fit inside
the shadow of the moon
or get to the next level, if

the monster is learned
the victims have multiplied, the
target has, start over. Here
are the rules of the game

~

how to pass the time in silence
when the arcade
is meant to be full
of noise is a paradox worth

sharing, then a customer comes
in, finally looks around
like, where's all the
flashing lights, chaos and

clanging coins, smiles and children
with flowing tails of tickets
like where did the sign say anything
about this place becoming a museum

Notes

(1) pg. 3: This poem is based on the beginning of Jean Baudrillard's *Simulacra and Simulation* (1981).

(2) pg. 6: "if I could, I'd annex other planets" was said by Cecil Rhodes, British mining magnate, imperialist, and politician. In 1895, Rhodes "founded" the southern African territory Rhodesia (now Zimbabwe and Zambia), which was named after him.

(3) pg. 10: A papoola, from the Philip K. Dick novel, *The Simulacra*, is an animal-like drone controlled by a human that sells products by mind control to passers-by.

(4) pg. 10: The italic parts were said by Margaret Atwood. I can't remember the source.

(5) pg. 19: This poem is based on Guillermo Parra's translation of an Emilio Adolfo Westphalen poem.

(6) pg. 21: This poem is based in part on the video game *Time Soldiers* developed in 1987 in Japan by Alpha Denshi.

(7) pg. 25: Momina Babi, a Pakistani grandmother and midwife, was killed by a drone strike while picking okra in a field with her grandchildren. From *The Bureau of Investigative Journalism*: "since 2002, there have been a minimum of 14,040 U.S. military drone strikes in Afghanistan, Pakistan, Yemen and Somalia. 8,858–16,901 people have been killed. Of the dead, up to 2,200 have been civilians. 283–454 have been children." This data has not been updated in some time, so the numbers are much higher than this.

(8) pg. 26: Out of desperation, Palestinians and other victims of technologically advanced military attacks, have thrown or sling-shotted stones at tanks and drones.

(9) pg. 27: In the documentary *Drone* (Dir. Tonje Hessen Schei, 2014), Brandon Bryant, a former drone operator tells the story of his first fatal drone strike. The Safety Observer counts down to zero as the Hellfire missile hits a human being and yells, "Splash!" He laughs, slaps Bryant on the back and says, "you should have seen how you jumped when I said, "Splash."

(10) pg. 29: Solitary confinement is the practice of isolating people in closed cells for 22-24 hours a day, virtually free of human contact, for periods of time ranging from days to decades. From *Solitary Watch*: "The number of people held in solitary confinement in the United States is notoriously difficult to determine. The lack of reliable information is due to state-by-state variances and shortcomings in data gathering and ideas of what constitutes solitary confinement. Currently available estimates suggest that at least 80,000 men, women, and children are held in some form of isolated confinement on any given day."

(11) pgs. 31 & 35: "secrets of the state," "more hormones" alludes to Chelsea Manning, a transgender woman and United States' soldier who was imprisoned for violating the Espionage Act and other offenses. She leaked 750,000 classified and sensitive documents as a whistleblower to the journalist outlet, WikiLeaks. While in jail, she began hormone replacement therapy, and part of her time was spent in solitary confinement. President Obama commuted her 35-year sentence in 2017.

(12) pg. 33: The Jungle refers to a refugee camp located on a former landfill site near Calais, France, where migrants from Syria, Palestine, Eritrea, Iraq, Afghanistan, Egypt, Sudan, Somalia, and other war-torn and unstable nations were attempting to enter the United Kingdom.

(13) pg. 34: In a 2010 interview Matt Lauer asked President George W. Bush, "Why is waterboarding legal in your opinion"? Bush responded, "Because the lawyer said it was legal. He said it did not fall within the Anti-torture Act. I'm not a lawyer, but you gotta trust the judgment of people around you, and I do."

(14) pg. 37: "six by eight walls that close to a crush" comes from what Albert Woodfox, one of the Angola three who spent almost 44 years in solitary confinement, said about such torture: "It takes so much out of you just to try to make these walls, you know, go back to the normal place they belong…" Woodfox and Herman Wallace were convicted of killing a prison guard in 1972 with no physical evidence and unreliable witnesses. Woodfox still claims his innocence and said he and Wallace were set-up because they were Black Panthers. Woodfox was finally released from prison in February 2016. Wallace was released from jail in 2013 and died soon after from liver cancer. He spent 40 years in solitary confinement. Robert King is the third of the Angola 3, released from jail in 2001 after 29 years in solitary confinement.

(15) pg. 47: Language from the first stanza is found language from the GQ

article titled "Confessions of a Drone Warrior" (2013) by Matthew Power.

(16) pg. 49: foma comes from the fictionalized religion of Bokononism from Kurt Vonnegut's *Cat's Cradle*.

(17) pg. 52: "Exit light" and "take my hand…" are lyrics from the Metallica song, "Enter Sandman." The U.S. military has used Metallica songs as sound disorientation torture on prisoners. Other music used as torture: Eminem, Rage Against the Machine, AC/DC, Christina Aguilera, David Gray, Tupac, Bruce Springsteen, and even the theme song from Sesame Street.

(18) pg. 53: These are all the names of military unmanned air vehicles or drones.

(19) pg. 58: The burnt orange prescription bottle comes from John Ashbery.

(20) pg. 59: Genre breakdown of video game sales in the United States in 2018 comes from Statista.

(21) pg. 65: Except for a few changed words, this poem is a found poem from McKenzie Wark's book Gamer Theory, 2007 (pg. 26).

(22) pg. 65: These are all some of the top-rated first-person shooter games on the market.

(23) pg. 66: In *Joystick Nation* (1997), J.C. Herz said, "Lockheed Martin may be beating digital ploughshares into swords, but most of the technology that's now used in video games had its origins in military research. When you trace back the patents, it's virtually impossible to find an arcade or console component that evolved in the absence of a Defense Department grant. It's easy to forget, when you're constantly playing say, a Game Boy, that the twenty-year old technology in its silicon guts was originally financed by the Pentagon.

(24) pg. 69: "push murder paper around all day" comes from Holly Michelle Wood, aka girlziplocked, a blogger and social media voice. She's specifically speaking about United States' politicians (medium.com).

(25) pg. 70: According to Airforce Times, Drone Operators can receive an expanded $175,000 retention bonus ($35,000/year over 5 years) if they agree to a 5-year active-duty service commitment. Brandon Bryant was offered a similar bonus as his contract was about to expire. He refused the bonus and exited the military.

(26) pg. 70: LIBOR stands for London Interbank Offered Rate, the rate of interest at which banks offer to lend money to one another in the wholesale money markets in London. It was discovered in 2012 that many big banks falsely inflated or deflated their rates to profit from trades or give the impression that they were more solvent than they were. Guilty banks: Barclays, UBS, Rabobank, Citigroup, The Royal Bank of Scotland, Deutsche Bank, JPMorgan, Lloyds, and others. Investigations are still pending. So far, nobody has gone to jail. After the scandal, the Secured Overnight Financing Rate (SOFR) replaced LIBOR, as it is based on observable transactions rather than estimated borrowing rates.

(27) pg. 71: These are all automated programs that mine through data on the Internet.

(28) pg. 72: "Battlespace," "around-the-clock tracking," "persistent stare," "unblinking eye," and "find, fix, finish" are all military terms connected to drone surveillance. I discovered them while reading "The Drone Papers" in The Intercept.

(29) pg. 73: Some families whose children were killed during drone attacks have protested such atrocities by covering their roofs with enlarged pictures of their deceased children for the drone operators to see as they fly overhead.

Acknowledgments

I'm grateful to the editors at the following journals/anthologies in which these poems first appeared:

Texas Review, Fall 2022: "the drone operator flies along," "the operator refuses," "good banking is good citizen," "terror as an assembly line," "I confess to you my sins"
Rabid Oak, April 2022: "twenty-three hours in solitary"
Matter Sept. 2021: "a cloud that follows us"
Yes Poetry, May 2021: "an app to colonize the stars," "the future is here, and it's"
Cartridge Lit, March 2021: "an odyssey, in arcade years," "maybe we're all just time soldiers," "the difference between death and," "to build an arcade is simple," "we've come a long way since spacewar!"
Drunken Boat/Meridian Anthology, Dec. 2020: "when astronomers say we're not far," "around the corner we will all," "in the world that does exist," "the split body, parts," "enough with positive thinking"
Epigraph Magazine, Sept. 2020: "the prisoner is a hologram," "living room cockpits of complicity," "glory (hole) for the theophany," "in solitary, research proves," "the prisoner in a t-shirt," "the sky and ocean are reverses"
8 Poems, May 2020: "the contestant enters but what she thinks"
Everything in Aspic, Winter 2020: "I'm still utterly terrifyingly human" and "stark, dark, unforgettable"
DIAGRAM, Winter 2020: "if the operator enters the drone" and "strange electronic limbo, white"
POETiCA REViEW, Fall 2019: "crosses loomed over the roman,"
Juked, Fall 2019: "let's invite the monster, a heartache may follow," "the enemy is a monster," and "the operator's feed is too grainy"
Pretty Owl Poetry, Summer 2019: "bubbling above the waves, god's voice," "saturn posseses a moon that may contain," "the contestant was abducted," "the contestant thinks the world," and "because women are interesting"
Word For/Word, Summer 2019: "in the river, what rises in the river," "the operator thought it was the coolest," "in the control room, a picture," "secret patterns of behavior," "six thousand twenty year olds," "do you hear that buzz around,"
Guacamole Literature Magazine, Apr. 2015: "if a bank crashes," "flatten your hand," "weary of make believe," "in the river," and "there's a sucker born"
Jubilat, January 2015: "all these children leaving the arcade,"
Called Back Books, The Sampler, Summer 2014: "Self-Portrait with Oranges"
The New People, Mar. 2013: "the drone operator is sick,"
Whiskey and Fox, Nov. 2011: "I think money's been a really a disappointing thing"

Thank you to all who helped and inspired me to create this book, especially Emily Carlson, Sten Carlson, Meg Shevenock, Daniel C. Remein, Ian Finch, Stephanie Ford, Faith Barrett, Joy Katz, Rita Mockus, Colby Gillette, LM Rivera, and Elizabeth Jones Hanley. Thanks to my teachers: Kate Northrop, Lynn Emanuel, Toi Derricotte, Paul Kameen, Kim Addonizio, Michael Donaghy, Mark Jarman, and Carolyn Sorisio. Anything I ever write that is good is because of Tomaž Šalamun—the best teacher of all. Thanks to Toi Derricotte for her careful reading, insightful commentary, and encouragement; to Brenda Hillman for her generous reading, advice, and guidance seeking publishers; and Charles Legere for his thoughtful, critical feedback. Thank you to Bradley J. Fest for introducing me to *Gamer Theory,* McKenzie Wark's brilliant work. Thank you to the English Departments at the University of Pittsburgh (where I got my MFA), Carnegie Mellon University, and Duquesne University. Thank you to the West Chester University Poetry Conference where I learned you could go to graduate school to write poetry among a community of poets. Thank you to my dear students and colleagues at Colfax and the Student Achievement Center (PPS Schools). Thank you to the fine folks at Finishing Line Press who took a chance on publishing this incendiary book—with a special shout out to Jackie Steelman, my editor Christen Kincaid, and publisher Leah Maines. Julie Granum, your memory is always with me. Thank you to nonpolygon (Ian Finch) for his striking art and design work for the cover of the book. Thank you to my family: Erik, Mom, Dad, Jason, Caroline, Shawn, Stacey, Shannan, Dave, Johnny, Carter, Joey, Luke, Lila, Danny, Zoe, Julianne, and Emmy for your love and encouragement. This book would not have found its form and function to its fullest potential without the close readings, insights, edits, and revision suggestions of my dear beloved partner, Robin Clarke who is usually always right. Charlotte and Violet, you are my two favorite human beings in all za world. Big koala hugs to both of you! This book has been written with immeasurable memoriam.

Joshua Zelesnick writes poetry and essays and fiddles around on the guitar or ukelele most evenings, likely and preferably with his two kids playing nearby or hanging on him. Born and raised in Downingtown, Pennsylvania, he earned his B.S. from West Chester University and MFA from the University of Pittsburgh.

His debut poetry collection, *Insert Coin* (Finishing Line Press, 2025) was a finalist for the Marystina Santiestevan First Book Prize at Conduit Books and Ephemera and the Trio Award at Trio House Press. *Cherub Poems*, his chapbook, was published with Bonfire Books in 2019. His poetry and prose have appeared widely in magazines and journals including Diagram, The Texas Review, Jubilat, Juked, Labor Notes, and Counterpunch. He's currently working on a poetry book titled *Very Beautifully, Suddenly*.

Zelesnick has taught writing at Carnegie Mellon University, University of Pittsburgh, Duquesne University, and the Community College of Allegheny County, and is currently a Librarian and creative writing teacher with Pittsburgh Public Schools. While at Duquesne, he helped start a union for part-time faculty in the McAnulty College that the administration at the school never recognized even after faculty won a legally stipulated election.

He lives in Pittsburgh, PA with his loving partner and kids in a garden co-housing community. With friends, he helps host a living-room music and reading series.

www.ingramcontent.com/pod-product-compliance
Lightning Source LLC
Chambersburg PA
CBHW020337170426
43200CB00006B/422